Preface

I have used the Spanish spelling in the title and contents of this book. Strictly speaking, the English is Majorca, but I decided that Mallorca is in more popular use.

I fell in love with Mallorca and its gastronomy many years ago and one of my enduring pleasures is finding hidden gems of restaurants or a new artisan producer. Indeed, I could wax long and lyrical about the island, but the purpose of this book is to help you reproduce Mallorcan dishes in your own home, using ingredients which are easy, or at least not too difficult, to find.

Where appropriate, the recipes are in Mallorquin, Castilian Spanish, and English.

Bon Profit!

Introduction

It is fair to say that Mallorcan cuisine is unique, but it is equally fair to say that it reflects a combination of influences over hundreds of years – Roman, Moorish, Catalan, and general Spanish.

Your Mallorcan store cupboard will not require very much out of the ordinary, especially if you are already familiar with Spanish cooking. If you want to be really authentic, many Mallorcan foods are available from specialist delicatessen or online suppliers. Mallorcan almonds, olive oil and sea salt are of the highest quality. It is also possible to obtain *galletes d'oli*, the small, hard savoury biscuits, often flavoured with rosemary.

However, for the most part, produce from your usual shop or supermarket or imported from mainland Spain will be fine and there will be no discernible difference in the finished dish. One notable exception is *sobrasada*, which features in quite a few recipes in this book and is virtually indispensable in Mallorcan cookery.

Traditionally, Mallorcan food is cooked in a terracotta dish called a *greixonera*. It feels and looks great, especially when served at the table, but for practical purposes, your normal cookware will be perfectly adequate.

Mallorcan food in general is not the prettiest – its beauty lies within. It is rarely a photogenic choice for Facebook or Instagram and when you bring a dish to the table, your family and friends will not shout "Wow!", but when they taste it, you will see them smile in silent satisfaction.

There are some first-rate chefs on the island, like Marc Fosh, Adrián Quetglas and Andreu Genestra for example, but this book is not about them or haute cuisine in general, but hearty peasant food made from good ingredients with love and passion.

" It could perfectly well have been Majorca that the little chimney sweep in the story was describing when he said, in praise of the inn, that it sold five kinds of meat: hog, boar, swine, pig, bacon, and ham. I am certain that Majorca boasts more than two thousand dishes prepared with pig meat. "

George Sand, 1841

Bread

Bread has been a staple in Mallorca since Roman times and there are still a few bakeries using traditional wood-fired ovens. The traditional cob-type loaves, *pa de pagès* or *pa moreno* are dense and full-flavoured with a robust crust. *Pa moreno*, the brown version, is sliced and used in *sopes* (see recipes).

At home, of course, you can use any bread of your choice, but especially for *pa amb oli*, try to find a good solid country loaf with a nice crust.

Almonds

One of the greatest sensory pleasures of rural Mallorca is seeing the acres of pink and white almond blossom in spring. Mallorcan almonds have PGI status, but may be difficult to find elsewhere, so you can substitute a good quality almond like Marcona.

Olives and Pickles

Mallorcan green olives can be something of an acquired taste as the first stage of curing is omitted, causing them to be quite hard and bitter. They are usually split – *trencada* – and often cured with fennel, or garlic and chilli.

The black olives, *pansides*, are fully ripe and usually stored in olive oil and salt.

They can both be found at specialist importers, but otherwise, the closest thing to the green is probably *verdial* and to the black, *empeltre*.

Fonoll Marí or sea fennel is a popular accompaniment in Mallorca, especially with pa amb oli. It is actually rock samphire and grows wild on the cliffs around the coast. It is collected and pickled in vinegar, sometimes with a little salt. It is produced commercially and can sometimes be found at an importer, but an alternative is to use the much more readily available marsh samphire (also known as sea beans, sea asparagus or glasswort) and pickle it at home. Clean, blanch and cool the samphire, then put it in a sterilized jar and cover with white vinegar – you can use white wine, cider or sherry vinegar if you like. Add any herbs or spices of your choice and store it in the 'fridge for up to three weeks.

Olive Oil

Like wine, the production and availability of olive oil in Mallorca has grown exponentially over the last few years. Also like wine, the emphasis is on quality rather than quantity and most of the oils are exceptionally good, PDO status being awarded in 2002. Only a few are made with the autochthonous *mallorquina* olive, most producers preferring *arbequina* or *picual*. At the time of writing, only a few varieties are exported, but there should be no difficulty in finding some.

Sea Salt

Mallorca has its own sea salt, Flor de Sal d'Estrenc, harvested by hand in the south-east of the island. It comes in various flavours and is now generally available.

Sobrasada

Sobrasada (*sobrassada* in Mallorquin) is a soft spreadable sausage with a multitude of uses. *Sobrasada de Mallorca* has PGI protected status

and is made from the meat of the local porc negre, or 'black pig', which is related to the ibérico pig of the mainland, but is slightly larger with a longer neck.

Firstly, the pork is minced to a quite fine texture, to which pimentón, salt and spices (such as pepper, rosemary, thyme and oregano) are added. The mixture is mechanically kneaded into a dough, which is then stuffed into natural gut.

The second stage, curing, is carried out in drying sheds, where the product will be cured for up to six months (depending on its size), to obtain the product's unique characteristics. It is available in a choice of either mild or spicy.

It is often simply spread on bread or toast, but it can be fried in slices or melted into casseroles. It can make a fabulous sauce, especially with honey, and its versatility even lends itself to desserts in Mallorca – try it with fresh figs or baked apple.

At the time of writing, genuine sobrasada is not available in the US, but an acceptable substitute can be found or failing that a fake Italian nduja will do the job.

Beer and Wine

Mallorca is home to quite a community of craft brewers (see *The Beers of Mallorca, Cornucopia Books/Amazon*), but unfortunately the beers very rarely leave the island.

Mallorcan wines, however, can often be obtained from specialist suppliers. When I first started visiting Mallorca regularly in the late 80s and 90s, there were eight wineries (and no breweries) and now there are upwards of fifty vineyards. Because of the scale of production and transport costs, they do tend to be relatively expensive, but they are worth trying.

The two best known Mallorcan liqueurs, both digestifs, are Hierbas (*Herbes* in Mallorquin) and Palo. Again, they are not often found outside Mallorca, but you may be fortunate enough to come across a bottle.

Hierbas, as its name implies, is made from a mixture of herbs with an aniseed base and comes in sweet (dulce), dry (seco or seques), or mezcladas (mesclades), mixed.

Palo is a dark, bitter-sweet drink made with quinine and gentian.

Pa amb Oli

Pa amb Oli means bread and oil and at its simplest, that's what it is, but in Mallorca it's much, much more. It's not just a popular dish, but has become something of a cultural icon. Indeed, Tomás Graves has written a very informative and entertaining book on the subject – *Bread & Oil: Majorcan Culture's Last Stand* (Prospect/Grub Street).

It is usually made with the dense local country bread, sometimes lightly toasted, then rubbed with garlic and scrubbed with tomato. In Mallorca, the ramellet or hanging tomato is used, but a good ripe vine tomato will suffice. It is then doused with olive oil, or indeed, it may be the other way round. A fierce debate surrounds this. Some say that if the tomato is applied first, the oil will not soak in, whilst others aver that if the oil is first, the tomato will not scrub properly, so it really is a matter of choice. It is then sprinkled with a little sea-salt and is frequently topped with ham and cheese and served with olives and pickles.

FIRA
DEL
PA
AMB
OLI

El millor Pa amb Oli del Món

Del 28 de Febrer al 3 de Marc,
amb motiu del Dia de les Illes Balears
al Parc de Sa Feixina.
28 de Febrer celebració del
I Campionat del Món de Pa amb Oli.

Over time, bars and restaurants have vied with each other for the most interesting topping and this has resulted in the World Pa amb Oli Championship, held in Palma on the Balearic National Day in March. Once, I tried the winner which was topped with cheese and peix sec, a type of dried fish from Formentera, but I actually preferred the runner-up which was deep-fried cod with red pepper and a sweet tomato sauce.

It is such a local institution that when I once ate at a restaurant in Petra, they had a long and impressive list of accompaniments for their pa amb oli. I chose what was probably the most outrageous – lamb cutlets – which were delicious, but definitely considered to be secondary to the pa amb oli.

A Note on Measures

As far as possible, ingredients are given in grams and ounces. A teaspoon is 5ml/g or approximately 0.2 oz/fluid oz. A spoon is a dessert spoon, 10ml/g or approximately 0.4 oz/fluid oz. A tablespoon is 15ml/g or approximately 0.6 fluid oz.

There are minor variations between Imperial and US measurements, but with these recipes it should not present a problem. However, as a general principle, whether using metric, Imperial or US, it is best to stick with the same in any given dish.

Recipes

16

Gato page 84
Tarta de Almendras/Almond Cake

Flam de Taronja page 86
Flan de Naranja/Orange Flan

Some of the following recipes call for lard. Mallorcan lard is pork lard, which is naturally soft and creamy. If pork lard is not available, you can use beef lard (tallow), butter, or vegetable shortening.

Trempó
Ensalada Mallorquina/Mallorcan Salad

Trempó or *trampó* is a simple summer salad and the ingredients are variable. Red peppers, garlic, apple and apricot are often added or substituted. Buy the best and freshest ingredients possible and choose a good quality oil, perhaps a single varietal.

Serves 4

1 medium onion, finely sliced
4 large salad tomatoes, finely chopped
1 spring onion, trimmed, peeled and chopped
2 green peppers, cored, de-seeded and diced
olives (optional)
capers (optional)
1 tablespoon of red wine vinegar (optional)
4 tablespoons of extra virgin olive oil
1 pinch of sea salt

Mix all the ingredients in a bowl and stir the salt through.

Add the vinegar if using and then ensure that the ingredients are well coated with olive oil.

Serve with pickles and crusty bread.

Tumbet
Cazuela de Berenjenas/Vegetables in Olive Oil

Very similar to ratatouille except for the use of potatoes, there are many recipes for tumbet. It is served as a starter, side dish or occasionally as a more substantial dish with the addition of eggs, fish or meat, like slices of fried pork loin.

Serves 4

½kg/1lb of aubergines (2 medium-sized), sliced into rounds
½kg/1lb of potatoes, peeled and sliced
½kg/1lb of red peppers, cored and de-seeded
1 kg/2lbs of tomatoes, skinned and chopped
1 medium sized courgette, sliced
3 cloves of garlic, peeled and chopped
large pinch of sea salt
large pinch of ground black pepper
¼litre/8fl oz/I cup of olive oil

Lightly salt the aubergine slices, leave for half an hour and then rinse with cold water. Pat dry.

Heat the oil in a frying pan and separately cook the potatoes, aubergine, courgette and peppers, removing each at a time and leaving to drain on absorbent paper.

In the same pan, fry the garlic and tomatoes to make a thick sauce and season with salt and pepper.

Arrange the vegetables in layers beginning with potato, then aubergine, courgette and peppers in an ovenproof dish or casserole, sprinkling each layer with a little salt.

Pour the sauce over the vegetables and bake in a hot oven for thirty minutes.

Coca

There is no real translation for coca. Pastry is inadequate, but so is tart, flatbread, pie or indeed, cake. It is often likened to a pizza, though Mallorcans would not thank you for that comparison. There are many combinations of toppings including swiss chard, aubergine (eggplant) or just peppers. They can be served hot or cold.

Cocas can be round, square or rectangular. This recipe will provide enough dough to fill a baking tray of approximately 34cm/14" diameter.

For the dough:

250g/9oz of plain/all-purpose flour
25g/1oz of lard, cut into small pieces
15g/½oz of fresh yeast
1 pinch of salt
135ml/5fl oz of warm water
1 tablespoon of olive oil

Dissolve the yeast in the warm water, then stir in the lard and the olive oil. Leave in a warm place for ten to fifteen minutes.

Sift the flour and salt into a large bowl and make a well in the centre. Pour in the yeast mixture gradually, mixing constantly.

Knead well – if sticky, add more flour and if too stiff, add water. When it is smooth and elastic, return to the bowl, cover with a cloth and leave for an hour or two to rise.

Knead again and the dough is ready. Grease the baking tray and roll the dough.

Spread evenly and press unto the baking tray. It is now ready for the topping.

Coca de Trampó
Torta de Verduras/Vegetable Pastry

3 green peppers, cored, de-seeded and cut into pieces
500g/1lb of ripe tomatoes, thinly sliced
1 large white onion, thinly sliced
1 clove of garlic, peeled and finely chopped
1 tablespoon of flat-leaf parsley, finely chopped
1 teaspoon of pimentón dulce (mild smoked paprika)
1 pinch of salt
1 tablespoon of olive oil

Mix the vegetables, pimentón, salt and half the olive oil in a bowl.

Spread evenly on top of the dough and bake in a moderate oven for about forty-five minutes or until the dough and toppings are cooked.

Remove from the oven and sprinkle with the remaining olive oil.

Coca amb Llom i Pebres
Torta con Lomo de Cerdo y Pimientos/Pork Loin and Pepper Pastry

8 slices of pork loin, cut into pieces
1kg/2lbs 4oz of red and green peppers
3 cloves of garlic, peeled and finely chopped
1 tablespoon of flat-leaf parsley, finely chopped
1 pinch of salt
1 tablespoon of olive oil

Grill or roast the peppers until blackened, then cool and remove the skin and seeds. Cut into pieces and mix in a bowl with the other ingredients and half the olive oil.

Spread evenly on top of the dough and bake in a moderate oven for about forty-five minutes or until the dough and toppings are cooked.

Remove from the oven and sprinkle with the remaining olive oil.

Sopes
Sopas Mallorquinas/Mallorcan Bread and Cabbage

More of a cabbage stew, the word *sopes* does not mean soup, but actually refers to the slices of dry country bread, which are sold pre-prepared in bags in Mallorca. An acceptable substitute can be made by taking thin slices of day-old brown bread and allowing them to dry, covered, for another 24 -48 hours.

This is a basic recipe for sopes, but there are versions for summer and winter and some might include cauliflower, peas, artichoke, spinach or even asparagus and *sopes de matances* has the addition of pork.

Serves 4

1 small or half a large white cabbage, centre removed and cut into strips
200g/8oz of prepared bread slices
1 large onion, chopped
2 large ripe tomatoes, skinned and chopped
2 cloves of garlic, finely chopped
1 teaspoon of pimentón dulce (mild smoked paprika)
1 small handful of flat-leaf parsley, chopped
large pinch of sea salt
3 tablespoons of olive oil

In a stockpot or earthenware dish, fry the onion, garlic and tomato in olive oil until softened and amalgamated.

Add the shredded cabbage, paprika and salt. Add enough water to cover and simmer for around thirty minutes until the cabbage is cooked and most of the water absorbed.

In an earthenware dish or separate soup bowls, place a layer of bread, sprinkle with olive oil, top with the vegetables and repeat. Leave for a couple of minutes for the bread to absorb the juices and serve, garnished with the parsley.

Pancuit
Sopa de Ajo/Garlic Soup

Many Mediterranean countries have their version of garlic soup and this is the Mallorcan one. It is quite thick, almost like a stew, but, of course, the amount of liquid can be varied to suit.

Serves 4

12 cloves of garlic, peeled and crushed
100g/3.5oz of stale rustic bread
3 teaspoons of pimentón (smoked paprika)
1.5L/36fl oz of water
3 free range eggs, beaten
150ml/5fl oz of olive oil
1 pinch of sea salt

Fry the garlic in hot oil until golden, then add the water, pimentón and salt.

Crumble in the bread, bring to the boil and simmer for about ten minutes.

Remove the pan from the heat, stir the eggs through and serve immediately.

Panades d'Anyell
Empanadas de Cordero/Lamb Pies

Traditionally made at Easter, these pies are now enjoyed all year round. They can be eaten hot or cold.

Makes 10 – 12 pies

For the pastry:

500g/1lb of plain/all-purpose flour
75g/2½oz of lard
1 egg yolk, beaten
125ml/4½fl oz of olive oil
125ml4½ of water
1 pinch of salt

For the filling:

500g/1lb of boned lamb shoulder, cut into small cubes
200g/7oz of sobrasada
100g/3½oz of streaky bacon, cut into pieces
150g/6oz of peas
½ teaspoon of pimentón dulce (mild smoked paprika)
1 pinch of black pepper
1 pinch of sea salt
dash of olive oil

Firstly, season the peas with oil, pimentón, salt and pepper.

Mix all the ingredients for the dough except the flour in a bowl. Add the flour little by little until you obtain a smooth dough, but do not knead excessively.

Take a small handful (about 75g/2½oz) of the dough and make a small pot with a base of about 10 cm/4" in diameter and a wall of 3-4 cm/1-1½".

Place some peas in the bottom, then cover with a few pieces of bacon followed by sobrasada, lamb and finally a few peas again.

Roll some dough and make a round lid for the pot, folding and crimping the edges together.

Prick the lid with a fork so that the steam can escape and bake at 190°c for about forty-five minutes until the pastry is golden.

Cocarrois
Pastelitos de Verduras/Vegetable Pasties

Cocarrois are sometimes made with spinach, which may be substituted for the Swiss chard. Extra fillings can include onion, spring onion, and chicory. They can be eaten hot or cold.

Makes 10 – 12 pasties

For the pastry:

500g/1lb of plain/all-purpose flour
75g/2½oz of lard
1 egg yolk, beaten
125ml/4½fl oz of olive oil
125ml4½ of water
1 pinch of salt

For the filling:

½ cauliflower, cut into tiny florets
1 bunch of Swiss chard
1 tablespoon of raisins
1 tablespoon of pine nuts
1 teaspoon of pimentón (mild smoked paprika)
1 pinch of sea salt
1 pinch of black pepper
dash of olive oil

Mix all the ingredients for the dough except the flour in a bowl. Add the flour little by little until you obtain a smooth dough, but do not knead excessively.

Roll out on a floured surface and cut into rounds of approximately 12cm/5" diameter. Wash and shred the Swiss chard, discarding the thick part of the stems. Mix in a bowl with the cauliflower florets, raisins and pine nuts and toss with the oil, pimentón, salt and pepper.

Place a spoonful of the mixture in the centre of a pastry circle, dampen the edges and draw them upwards to form a ridge, sealing and crimping together to form the traditional pattern.

Bake at 190°c for about forty-five minutes until the pastry is golden.

Samoses Mallorquines amb Sobrassada
Samosas Mallorquinas con Sobrasada/Mallorcan Samosas with Sobrasada

East meets West with this delightful snack. Sobrasada and honey go perfectly together and this little tapa can be served on its own or as part of a spread. They are best eaten straight away, but can be carefully frozen if only cooked half way, then finished off when needed.

Makes 10 - 12 samosas.

300g/10oz sobrasada
1 small aubergine, peeled
1 large shallot, peeled
1 pack of filo pastry
1 tablespoon olive oil
1 pinch of sea salt
1 pinch of black pepper
1 tablespoon of runny honey
melted butter

Chop the aubergine and shallot into small pieces and sauté in the olive oil with the salt and pepper until they form a homogenous mixture.

Drain and allow to cool, then mix well with the sobrasada.

Lay the filo pastry flat and cut in half lengthwise.

Take two sheets of pastry and place a small spoonful of the mixture about 2cm up from the bottom edge, towards one side. Take a corner of the pastry and fold it over to make a triangle, covering the filling. Fold over again and continue folding in triangles until you reach the end of the strip. Brush around the samosa with melted butter, being sure to seal the edges.

Deep-fry, air-fry, or bake in the oven until golden. Remember to turn the samosas half way through.

Serve drizzled with honey.

Ous al Plat amb Sobrassada
Huevo al Horno con Sobrasada/Baked Egg with Sobrasada

As the egg cooks, the sobrasada will melt and permeate the dish. It works well in individual terracotta cazuelas, but it can be made in a larger ovenproof dish (increase the ingredients pro rata if necessary) and portioned. As an alternative, you can add par-boiled diced potatoes to the dish part-way through and allow them to crisp.

Serves 2

100g/4oz sobrasada, roughly chopped
1 medium white onion, chopped
2 cloves of garlic, chopped
1 can of chopped tomatoes
1 rasher of bacon, chopped
2 large free-range eggs
1 pinch of salt
1 pinch of black pepper
1 tablespoon of olive oil

Heat the oil in a frying pan and sauté the onion, garlic and bacon until the onion is translucent and the bacon crispy.

Add the tomatoes, salt and pepper and fry for a few minutes until the tomato is cooked.

Add the sobrasada and stir through. Tip the mixture into the cazuelas (or ovenproof dish).

Make an indentation in the centre and add the egg. Bake in a hot oven until the white is set, but the yolk still runny.

Arros Brut
Arroz Brut/Hunter's Rice

Traditionally, this hearty dish is made with whatever is available at the time and may include rabbit or hare, pigeon, thrush or quail, and snails. Near the coast, seafood may even be added. This recipe uses ingredients which are easy to find, but by all means, experiment.

The main difference between this and other rice dishes like paella is that it is more liquid and generally served in a deeper, ideally earthenware, dish.

Serves 4

300g/10oz of short grain rice such as Bomba, Calasparra, Arborio or Carnaroli
4 chicken thighs
200g/8oz of chicken breast, diced
200g/8oz of pork fillet, diced
50g/2oz of sobrasada
1 medium onion, finely chopped
2 cloves of garlic, peeled and chopped
2 artichokes, trimmed, choke removed, and sliced
100g/4oz of mangetout, topped and tailed
100g/4oz of green beans, sliced

1 large tomato, skinned and chopped
1 red pepper, cored and diced
100g/4oz of wild mushrooms, sliced if large
1 tablespoon of flat-leaf parsley, chopped
1 small red chilli, de-seeded and finely chopped
4 saffron stamens, crushed to a powder
1 teaspoon of pimentón (mild smoked paprika)
½ teaspoon of ground cinnamon
½ teaspoon of sea salt
½ teaspoon of ground black pepper
2 litres/68fl oz of chicken stock
2 tablespoons of olive oil

Heat the oil in a large stockpot and brown the meat, a little at a time, then set aside.

In the same oil, fry the onion until translucent, then add the garlic, tomato and red pepper. Stir well and simmer for another two minutes.

Return the meat to the pan with the salt. Stir, add the stock and simmer, covered, for about thirty minutes.

Add the rest of the vegetables and the mushrooms, simmer for five minutes and then add the rice. Stir, bring back to the boil, then simmer, uncovered for ten minutes.

Add the spices, chilli and sobrasada and cook for another ten minutes or until the rice is ready.

Calamarsets amb Salsa
Chipirones en Salsa/Baby Squid in Sauce

This dish is best made with *chipirones*, also known as *puntillitas* or *chopitos*, the very small baby squid that are normally sourced from southern Spain, but any small squid will suffice, or you could even use a large one cut into pieces.

Serves 4

650g/1lb 7oz of baby squid
6 spring onions, diced
4 cloves of garlic, sliced
40g/1.5oz of raisins
30g/1oz of pine nuts
100ml/3.4fl oz of white wine
300ml/10fl oz of water
1 tablespoon of olive oil
1 spoon of flat-leaf parsley, chopped
1 pinch of sea salt
1 pinch of white pepper
1 bay leaf

Clean the squid thoroughly, removing the spines if necessary, then sauté them in olive oil, seasoning with salt and pepper.

Add the spring onion, garlic, pine nuts, raisins and bay leaf.

Add the white wine, stirring gently.

Place in a stockpot, add the water and cook over a low heat for about twenty minutes.

Pica-Pica de Sípia
Pica Pica de Sepia/Cuttlefish in Spicy Sauce

Pica Pica is normally served as a tapa or part of a *variat*, mixed tapas served on the same plate. It is sometimes made with squid and if cuttlefish proves difficult to obtain, then squid may be substituted.

Serves 4 as a tapa/starter

500g/1lb 2oz of cuttlefish, cleaned and cut into 5cm/2" pieces
1 medium white onion, coarsely chopped
1 red pepper, chopped
2 cloves of garlic, peeled and crushed
200g/7oz of tomatoes, coarsely chopped (or small can of chopped tomatoes)
200m/7fl oz of white wine
1 teaspoon of pimentón dulce (mild smoked paprika)
1 bay leaf
1 pinch of sea salt
2 tablespoons of olive oil

Heat the oil in a large sauté pan or stockpot and fry the cuttlefish for about a minute, stirring constantly.

Add the onions and tomatoes and cook for a further three minutes.

Add the pepper, garlic, bay leaf, pimentón, salt and white wine. Stir well then cover and simmer on a low heat for about twenty minutes.

Serve with some fresh crusty bread.

Guisat de Anguila
Estofado de Anguila/Eel Stew

Mallorcan eels are found in the S'Albufera wetlands in the north of the island. At one time, they were a common sight in homes and restaurants, but now, even in Mallorca they are not as popular as they once were. It's a shame really, as they are tasty and quick and easy to cook. This is a typical old recipe.

Serves 4

1kg/2lbs 3oz of eels, cut into thick slices
2 medium potatoes, peeled and diced
4 tomatoes, skinned and diced
4 spring onions (scallions), chopped
4 cloves of garlic, peeled and finely chopped

100g/4oz of green beans, chopped
2 artichoke hearts, diced
½ tablespoon of flat-leaf parsley, chopped
80g/3oz of pine nuts
75ml/3fl oz of white wine
1 teaspoon of pimentón dulce (mild smoked paprika)
½ teaspoon of sea salt
½ teaspoon of black pepper
½ teaspoon of dried oregano
1 pinch of ground cinnamon
plain/all-purpose flour
3 tablespoons of olive oil

Lightly toast the pine nuts in a frying pan with a drop of oil or on a baking sheet in the oven. Set aside.

Heat half the oil in a frying pan. Coat the eel pieces in flour and fry until lightly browned. Set aside.

Heat the remaining oil in a stockpot and sauté the spring onions. Add the tomato, stir and then add the white wine.

Reduce by a third and then add the garlic, pine nuts, salt, herbs and spices. Stir then add the eel and vegetables to the pan.

Add sufficient water to cover then simmer, covered, for about twenty minutes or until the potatoes are cooked. Reduce if necessary.

Soller Bacallà
Bacalao de Soller/Cod Soller Style

This dish is traditionally made with *bacalao*, dried and salted cod, from which all moisture has been removed. Whilst it is obviously no longer required as a means of preservation, *bacalao* is still popular due to its unique flavour and texture. However, fresh cod or any similar white fish will be absolutely fine for this recipe. If you are using salt cod, it needs to be soaked for 24 hours, changing the water at least 4 times.

Serves 4

600g/1lb 5oz of (salt) cod
1 medium white onion, finely chopped
2 cloves of garlic, chopped
500g/1lb 2oz of woodland mushrooms, cut into strips
100g/4oz of grated cheese
1 teaspoon of plain/all-purpose flour
125ml/4½fl oz of milk
1 tablespoon of olive oil
1 spoon of flat-leaf parsley, finely chopped
1 pinch of ground cinnamon

Shallow-fry the cod or simmer in a little water until it is just cooked, then break it into even sized pieces and place on the bottom of an appropriately sized oven-proof dish, ideally earthenware.

In a large frying pan, sauté the onion and garlic in olive oil until the onion is translucent.

Add the mushrooms.

Add the flour and mix well, then add the milk and cook until it thickens slightly.

Mix in the parsley and cinnamon and then pour over the cod.

Sprinkle with the grated cheese and bake in the oven for twenty minutes.

Greixonera de Peix
Cazuela de Pescado/Fish Casserole

Monkfish works very well for this recipe, but if price is an issue, then any firm white fish will be fine. It is normally cooked and served in a *greixonera*, a quite deep, round terracotta casserole dish.

Serves 4

1kg/2lbs of firm white fish, cleaned and cut into thick slices
500g/1lb of fresh mussels, cleaned
25g/1oz of sobrasada
4 medium potatoes, peeled and cubed
1 medium onion, chopped
3 ripe tomatoes, skinned and chopped
2 cloves of garlic, peeled and chopped
200g/8oz of peas, fresh or frozen
half a lemon
120ml4fl oz of white wine
1 tablespoon of pine nuts
1 tablespoon of flat-leaf parsley, chopped
1 tablespoon of pimentón dulce (mild smoked paprika)
1 bay leaf
1 pinch of sea salt
1 pinch of ground black pepper
500ml/16fl oz/2cups of water
4 tablespoons of olive oil

Firstly, cook the mussels in the white wine and enough water to cover, with half the parsley. Simmer until the mussels open, then remove them and put aside, retaining the stock.

Heat the oil in an earthenware cooking pot and gently fry the onion and tomato to form a *sofregit**.

Add the pimentón, bay leaf, lemon, salt and pepper. Stir, then add the mussel stock and the potatoes. Cook for ten minutes.

Meanwhile, fry the sobrasada for a couple of minutes, then grind with the garlic, pine nuts and the rest of the parsley with a pestle and mortar or small food processor.

Add the fish and the peas to the cooking pot and simmer for a further ten minutes, adding a little water or stock if necessary.

Add the mussels and then stir the sobrasada mixture through, gently but thoroughly. Bring back to the boil, simmer very gently for five minutes and the dish is ready.

**sofregit* (or *sofrito*) is a simple base for many meals and is made by gently frying onion and tomato in a little olive oil until a paste is formed.

Frit Marisc
Frito de Pescado/Mallorcan Fried Fish

Often served as a tapa or starter, the ingredients are quite variable. Cuttlefish and octopus may be used, but it does require a firm white fish like monkfish. Peas are optional and green peppers and artichokes may be added.

Serves 4

200g/8oz of monkfish, cut into small pieces
200g/8oz of squid, cut into small pieces
100g/4oz of peeled prawns
8 mussels, cleaned and steamed
2 medium potatoes, cleaned and cut into small cubes
1 large red pepper, cored, de-seeded and diced
3 spring onions, trimmed and chopped
4 cloves of garlic, finely chopped
50g/2oz of peas
1 sprig of fennel
1 bay leaf
1 pinch of sea salt
1 pinch of black pepper
1 tablespoon of olive oil

Heat the oil in a large sauté pan or earthenware pot and fry the potatoes for a few minutes until browned. Set aside.

In the same pan, soften the red pepper, then add the spring onion, garlic, fennel, bay leaf, salt and pepper.

Stir for a couple of minutes, then add the monkfish, squid and prawns.

Cook, turning gently, for another three minutes or until the fish is cooked then return the potatoes, with the peas and mussels.

Stir and heat through thoroughly and the dish is ready to serve. If at any point the dish is looking dry, add a little water or stock.

Pollastre amb Ametlles i Bolets
Pollo con Almendras y Setas/Chicken with
Almonds and Wild Mushrooms

In Mallorca, foraging for wild mushrooms is a very popular pastime and there are a number of edible  varieties, but obviously, do not pick your own unless you know what you are doing. Any shop-bought mushrooms will be fine for this recipe. If you use moscatel or a PX sherry, the dish will be that much richer.

Serves 4

3 chicken fillets, approx. 250g/8oz each, cut into thick strips
300g/10 oz of wild (woodland) or oyster mushrooms, trimmed as necessary
1 large white onion, chopped
50g/2oz of sobrasada chopped into small pieces
3 garlic cloves, peeled and finely chopped
80g/3oz of ground almonds
90ml/3fl oz of white wine or sherry
250ml/8fl oz/1 cup of chicken stock
½ teaspoon of chopped thyme
1 pinch of sea salt
1 tablespoon of olive oil

Heat the oil in a large frying pan or earthenware dish. Brown the chicken pieces and set aside.

In the same pan, fry the onion and garlic.

When the onion is beginning to turn translucent, add the sobrasada and as it begins to melt, add the wine or sherry.

When the wine has reduced, add the mushrooms, thyme and salt.

Stir and cook for five minutes, then add the chicken stock and return the chicken to the pan with the almonds.

Bring to the boil and simmer gently for about fifteen minutes, stirring occasionally.

Reduce if necessary and serve.

Escaldums de Pollastre
Guison de Pollo/Fricassee of Chicken

There are a number of different recipes for escaldums. Some include tomatoes, whilst others maintain it is not traditional. Prunes and pine nuts are sometimes added and some do not have potatoes or serve them separately at the side. It is a popular dish at Christmas, when turkey is often substituted for the chicken.

Serves 4

approx 1.5kg/3lbs 5oz chicken, cut up into eight pieces.
1 medium onion, finely sliced
1 head of garlic, outer skin removed
400g/14oz of small (new or baby) potatoes
50g/2oz of whole blanched almonds
100ml/3½fl oz of white wine
50g/2oz of sobrasada
1 bay leaf
1 teaspoon of dried oregano
1 pinch of sea salt
1 pinch of ground black pepper
plain/all-purpose flour
2 tablespoons of olive oil
milk

Fry the almonds briefly in a drop of olive oil until just golden, then grind to a powder with the sobrasada with a pestle and mortar. Add a little milk to form a smooth paste.

Season and lightly flour the chicken pieces, then fry in hot olive oil in a stockpot or earthenware cooking pot to brown all over. Remove and set aside.

In the same oil, fry the onion and garlic and when the onion has softened, add the white wine, bay leaf and oregano, then return the chicken to the pan.

Add sufficient water to cover, then bring to the boil and simmer gently, covered, for thirty minutes.

Fry the potatoes in hot oil for a few minutes, then drain and add to the pan with the almond and sobrasada paste.

Stir and continue cooking for another ten minutes.

Anèc amb Sobrassada i Mel

Pechuga de Pato con Sobrasada y Miel/Duck Breast with Sobrasada and Honey

The sauce here is the classic partnership of sobrasada and honey and it goes exceptionally well with the tender duck breast.

Serves 2

2 duck breasts
50g/2oz of sobrasada
2 tablespoons of runny honey
1 tablespoon of olive oil

Heat the oil in a frying pan and cook the slices of duck to your liking - medium-rare is fine for duck; it does not have to be cooked through like chicken.

Meanwhile, break up the sobrasada and add to a saucepan with the honey. Stir over a gentle heat until the sobrasada melts and combines with the honey. Be careful not to overcook it, so that it remains soft.

Plate up the duck slices, add the sobrasada and honey mix, and serve with a garnish of your choice.

Conill amb Ceba
Conejo con Cebolla/Rabbit with Onions

Rabbit can be something of a Marmite dish – people either love it or hate it – and it can be difficult to find, but this recipe, which is very popular in Mallorca, is definitely worth trying. It can be enjoyed as soon as it is ready or re-heated later, when some say the flavour will have improved.

Serves 2

1 rabbit, cut into pieces
25g/1oz of sobrasada, sliced
1 kg/2lbs 3oz of white onion, sliced into thin rings
1 clove of garlic, peeled and chopped
100ml of white wine
1 pinch of sea salt
1 pinch of ground black pepper
1 pinch of cinnamon
1 clove
3 tablespoons of olive oil

Add the olive oil to a large frying pan and fry the sobrasada until it begins to brown.

Add the rabbit pieces and fry, turning until browned all over. Remove and set aside on a plate to catch the juices.

In the same oil, fry the onion, garlic and salt until the onion is softened and begun to turn golden.

Place the onion and garlic, together with the rabbit and its juices in a large stockpot or ideally, a deep earthenware casserole. Pour in the white wine and just enough water or stock to cover. Simmer on a low heat, covered, for about an hour.

About ten minutes before the rabbit is ready, add the black pepper, cinnamon and clove. If necessary, reduce the sauce to quite a thick consistency.

Croquetes de Sobrassada
Croquetas de Sobrasada/Sobrasada Croquettes

Croquettes are, of course, ubiquitous in Spain, but these delicious examples are made with Mallorcan sobrasada. If you want to save time, you can buy béchamel sauce mix in powder form or even ready-made in jars, but be sure that you have the right consistency for rolling the croquettes – you may need to thicken it a little.

Makes about 20 croquettes

For the filling:
200g/8oz of sobrasada at room temperature, cut or torn into small pieces
1 tablespoon of runny honey
1 garlic clove, crushed
100g/3½oz of plain/all-purpose flour
550ml/1 pint/2½ cups of milk
1 spoon of flat leaf parsley, chopped
½ a teaspoon of salt
½ a teaspoon of black pepper
4 tablespoons of olive oil

For the coating:
750g/1lb 10oz of plain/all-purpose flour
2 large eggs, beaten
4 tablespoons of breadcrumbs

Heat the oil in a saucepan and add the garlic. Cook for about a minute, then stir in the flour. Add the milk gradually, stirring continuously.

Add the sobrasada and honey and cook over a low heat, stirring continuously for about fifteen minutes until you have a quite thick, smooth sauce.

Stir in the parsley, salt and pepper and mix well.

Turn out into a flat dish, allow to cool, cover and store in the 'fridge for at least two hours, ideally overnight.

Mould the mixture into croquette shapes, then roll first in the flour, then the beaten egg and finally the breadcrumbs. Chill for about fifteen minutes.

You can fry them in about 2.5cm/1" of hot oil in a pan or in a deep-fat fryer until crisp and golden. Cook them a few at a time so as not to lower the temperature and when they are ready, drain them on absorbent paper.

Serve immediately with a dip of your choice.

Pilotes de Carn
Albóndigas/Meatballs

This is a standard recipe for meatballs, but there are quite a few variations around the island. It is not unusual to add herbs such as oregano, marjoram, thyme and often mint. There are even recipes containing ground almonds and saffron.

Makes about 6 portions

300g/11oz minced pork
300g/11oz minced beef
100g/4oz sobrasada
½ onion, finely chopped
2 garlic cloves, crushed
1 medium egg
handful of breadcrumbs
1 spoon of pimentón dulce (or mild paprika)
½ teaspoon of salt
½ teaspoon of black pepper
1 spoon of dried mixed herbs

Put all the ingredients in a bowl and work with your (clean!) hands until thoroughly mixed. The reason that the quantity for breadcrumbs is vague is that you want to achieve a meatball that is firm and won't fall apart, but not too dense, so begin with a smaller amount and add more as required.

Form the meatballs by rolling them in your palms. The easiest way to cook them is to deep-fry at 165°c, but with care, they can be done in a frying pan. Fry until golden brown and ensure that the centre is cooked.

They can be served with dips of your choice, or with one of the following sauces:

Traditional Tomato Salsa

You can blanche, peel and chop your own tomatoes if you like, but good quality tins are fine.

1 tablespoon of olive oil
4 cans of chopped tomatoes
1 white onion, roughly chopped
1 red onion, roughly chopped
1 large red pepper, roughly chopped
2 spoons of garlic purée (paste)
teaspoon of salt
½ teaspoon of black pepper
2 spoons of pimentón dulce (or mild paprika)
good pinch of fresh or dried parsley
50ml/1.75fl oz of medium sherry

Warm the olive oil in a large saucepan or stockpot and sauté the onions and peppers until soft, but not browned.

Add one can of tomatoes, the garlic, salt, pepper and pimentón, stir well and simmer for a couple of minutes.

Add the rest of the tomatoes, the sherry and parsley, cover and simmer on a low heat, stirring occasionally, for approximately one hour.

Serve the meatballs in the salsa.

If you like your salsa hot, you can add chilli powder or flakes either whilst it is cooking or before you use it.

Vegetables and White Wine

1 medium white onion, diced
1 clove of garlic, chopped
2 ripe tomatoes, peeled and diced
400g/14oz of new potatoes
4 small carrots, sliced
400g/14oz of woodland mushrooms, chopped
30g/1oz of blanched almonds, finely chopped
30g/1oz of pine nuts, toasted
75ml/3fl oz of white wine
1 tablespoon of olive oil

Sauté the garlic and onions in olive oil until the onion is translucent, then add the tomatoes and carrots.

Place in a pot with the meatballs, pour the white wine over and reduce slightly.

Add the potatoes and mushrooms and enough water or stock to cover.

Simmer for twenty to thirty minutes or until the potatoes are cooked, then add the nuts and stir.

Reduce if necessary and serve.

Parsley Sauce

1 tablespoon of flat-leaf parsley, finely chopped
100g/3½oz of white breadcrumbs
50g/2oz of blanched almonds, finely chopped
I litre/30fl oz of beef stock

Pour some of the stock over the breadcrumbs and mix.

Add the parsley, nuts and the rest of the stock and heat gently until all the ingredients are combined, but the sauce is not too thick.

Serve the meatballs in the sauce.

Llom de Porc amb Col
Lomo con Col/Pork with Cabbage

There are many variations of this dish in Mallorca. Sometimes the local mushrooms, *esclata-sang*, are added and an occasional recipe calls for the whole loin to be roasted, with the shredded cabbage leaves added afterwards. If you can get hold of some *botifarro* sausage, a slice can be added with the *sobrasada*.

Serves 4

500g/1lb 2oz of pork loin, sliced
400g/14oz of cabbage leaves
50g/2oz of sobrasada, sliced
2 medium onions, finely chopped
3 garlic cloves, peeled and finely chopped
2 tomatoes, skinned and finely chopped
1 tablespoon of pine nuts
1 tablespoon of raisins
1 teaspoon of pimentón dulce (mild smoked paprika)
1 pinch of sea salt
1 pinch of ground black pepper
3 tablespoons of olive oil

Trim the cabbage leaves and blanch in salted water for three minutes, then drain and lay flat.

Fry the pork loin slices and then place one on each of the cabbage leaves. Top with a slice of sobrasada, season and wrap up like a parcel, securing with a cocktail stick.

In the same pan, sauté the onion until soft, then add the garlic, tomato and pimentón. Stir and cook for a couple of minutes, then season and add the pine nuts and raisins.

Shred the remaining cabbage and place on the bottom of a stockpot or, ideally an earthenware cooking pot. Lay the cabbage parcels on top and then pour the sauce over, adding a little water or white wine until they are just covered.

Cover and simmer gently for about an hour. Remove the cocktail sticks before serving.

Porc amb Moniato

Cerdo con Batatas/Pork Fillet with Sweet Potatoes

Sweet potatoes are not as popular as they once were in Mallorca, but there are plenty of recipes, both sweet and savoury. This is a good example, with the combination of pork and sweet potato harmonising very nicely.

Serves 4

8 slices of pork loin
500g/1lb 2oz of sweet potato, peeled and sliced
1 medium onion, finely sliced
1 apple, peeled, cored and sliced
500ml/16fl oz/2 cups of chicken stock
1 tablespoon of brown sugar
large pinch of sea salt
large pinch of ground black pepper
dash of lemon juice
1 tablespoon of olive oil

In a bowl, mix together the sweet potato, onion, and apple and toss with the brown sugar, salt, pepper, and lemon juice.

Coat an ovenproof dish, ideally an earthenware casserole, with the olive oil and then place the sweet potato, onion and apple mix on the bottom.

Lay the pork fillets on top and pour the stock over.

Cover and bake in a moderate oven for forty-five minutes, removing the cover for the last ten minutes to allow the pork to brown.

Raoles de Porc amb Espinacs
Raoles de Cerdo con Espinacas/Pork and Spinach Patties

The great advantage of these tasty little patties is that they can be made in advance. They will keep for a day in a sealed container in the 'fridge or can be frozen, but try to ensure they don't stick together or they may break apart when you separate them.

Makes 4-6 tapas

500g/1lb of minced pork
3 rashers of rindless bacon, finely chopped
200g/8oz of spinach, washed
half a large onion, finely chopped
3 cloves of garlic, finely chopped or 1 spoon of garlic purée
1 free-range egg
½ teaspoon of salt
1 pinch of ground black pepper
1 teaspoon of pimentón dulce (mild smoked paprika)
1 teaspoon of dried parsley
olive oil, for frying

Heat the spinach in a pan with a drop of water until it is just cooked. When it has cooled, squeeze it to remove as much water as possible and set aside.

In a bowl, combine all the other ingredients and mix thoroughly.

Tear the spinach and add to the bowl, working evenly through the mixture.

Chill and then form small patties. They need to be thin enough to cook through, but thick enough to not fall apart. Don't worry about the shape, as they are meant to look rustic.

Fry in hot oil until golden brown – check that they are cooked in the centre.

Drain on absorbent paper and then serve with alioli or a dip of your choice.

Frit Mallorquí
Frito Mallorquin/Mallorcan Lamb Fry

Traditionally, this dish is made with lamb heart, liver and lungs which are collectively known as an *asadura*. These are readily available pre-packed in supermarkets in Mallorca, but partly because of the difficulty of obtaining the ingredients elsewhere and partly due to the frequent aversion to hearts and lungs, this recipe uses just liver.

It is frequently served as a starter or a tapa. A similar dish called *frit de matances* uses pork and pork liver.

Serves 4

1 kg/2lbs of lamb's liver, diced
½kg/1lb of potatoes, peeled and cut into small cubes or chips
1 medium white onion, finely sliced
8 cloves of garlic, unpeeled
1 red pepper, diced
6 spring onions, trimmed and chopped
4 bunches of fennel fronds or alternatively 1 fennel bulb, chopped
2 bay leaves
1 teaspoon of pimentón dulce (mild smoked paprika)
1 pinch of sea salt

1 pinch of white pepper
12 tablespoons of olive oil

Fry the potatoes in olive oil in a large frying pan or earthenware dish until soft. Remove, drain and set aside.

Fry the liver in the same oil until lightly browned and then add the onion and red pepper.

Cook for about ten minutes, then add the garlic, spring onions, fennel and bay leaves plus the salt, pepper and paprika. Cook for a further ten minutes, occasionally giving a gentle stir and then add the potatoes back. Mix them in well and when heated through, serve.

Xai a l'estil Mallorquí
Cordero a la Mallorquina/Mallorcan Lamb Stew

This traditional Mallorcan dish is redolent of the cuisine of the Moorish occupation, with the dried fruits and honey. It requires a long, slow cooking, but it is most definitely worth the wait.

Serves 6

I kg/2lbs of boneless lamb shoulder, cut into 3cm/1½" cubes
2 medium onions, diced
2 cloves of garlic, peeled and finely chopped
2 green peppers, diced
15 prunes (pitted)
40g/1½oz of raisins
50g/1¾oz of dried apricots, roughly chopped
20g/¾oz of flaked almonds
40g/1½oz of pine nuts
1 tablespoon of runny honey
1 teaspoon of brown sugar
350ml/12fl oz of red wine
85ml/3fl oz of brandy
1 tablespoon of red wine vinegar
½ teaspoon of saffron, crumbled
½ teaspoon of cinnamon
1 pinch of ground cloves
1 teaspoon of sea salt

½ teaspoon of ground black pepper
plain/all-purpose flour
3 tablespoons of olive oil
mint leaves, roughly torn, to garnish

Firstly, lightly toast the almonds and pine nuts separately. You can do this in a frying pan with a tiny drop of oil or on a baking sheet in the oven, but be careful not to burn them. Set aside.

Heat half the olive oil in a frying pan and cook the onion, garlic and green pepper for a few minutes until the onion is translucent and just beginning to caramelize. Set aside.

Season the lamb with salt and pepper and dust lightly with flour. Heat the remaining oil in a large stockpot and brown the lamb, a few pieces at a time, setting aside.

Deglaze the stockpot with the brandy, then add the wine and 350ml/12fl oz of water or stock. Bring to a boil, then return the lamb to the pan with the onion mixture and the remaining salt and pepper and stir to mix.

Cover the pan and simmer gently for about an hour, then mix in the prunes, raisins and apricots. Continue to cook for a further hour.

Meanwhile, with a pestle and mortar or small food processor, grind the almonds, brown sugar, saffron, cinnamon and cloves to make a *picada*. Add this to the stockpot with the red wine vinegar and honey and mix well.

Cook for a further five minutes and serve garnished with the pine nuts and mint leaves.

Postres

Postres/Desserts

Bunyols
Buñuelos/Fritters

This recipe is sometimes called *Bunyols de Vent* (puffs of air) and there are similar ones such as *Bunyols de Pomes* which is made with grated apple. *Bunyols de Forat*, which are donut shaped, are made with potato and *Bunyols de les Verges* also contain sweet potato.

200g/8oz of self-raising/self-rising flour
50g/2oz of white granulated sugar
250ml/9fl oz/1 cup of milk
4 free-range eggs
50ml/2fl oz of olive oil
1 pinch of salt
zest of a lemon
icing sugar for dusting
vegetable or olive oil for frying

Bring the milk to the boil in a saucepan and dissolve the sugar with the salt and the lemon zest. Gradually add the flour and the olive oil.

Blend until smooth and when the dough no longer sticks to the side of the pan, remove from the heat and allow to cool.

Add the eggs one at a time and stir to mix thoroughly.

Heat the oil in a deep pan or electric deep-fryer. The oil needs to be hot enough to cook the bunyols through, but not so hot that they burn on the outside.

Form round lumps of batter with a spoon and drop them into the oil, being careful not to overload the pan.

When the bunyols are golden, remove them from the pan, drain on kitchen paper and then roll them in the icing sugar and allow to cool.

Crespells

Mantecados Mallorquines/Mallorcan Shortbread

Crespells are a type of sweet shortbread and are particularly popular during the Easter festivities (Setmana Santa). They come in various different shapes including stars, hearts, flowers, and fish.

500g of plain/all-purpose flour
150g of white granulated sugar
2 egg yolks
100g of lard, softened
50ml of natural orange juice
50ml of olive oil
zest of half a lemon, grated
1 pinch of cinnamon
icing sugar for dusting

Combine all the ingredients except the flour in a bowl.

When thoroughly mixed, fold in the flour to form a dough, then leave in a cool place for an hour.

Roll out to a thickness of about 1cm/½" and use a pastry cutter to make the desired shapes.

Bake in a moderate oven for about fifteen minutes until lightly coloured.

Allow to cool and dust with icing sugar.

Gató
Tarta de Almendras/Almond Cake

Gató (not to be confused with Castilian *gato*, which means cat!) is a traditional moist almond cake which is popular all year round, but especially so at Christmas and Easter. You can use a hand whisk for this recipe, but an electric one will considerably cut down on time.

6 large free-range eggs
300g/11oz of ground almonds
300g/11oz of caster sugar
1 tablespoon of icing sugar
1 teaspoon of ground cinnamon
zest of a lemon, finely grated

Firstly, separate the egg yolks and whites.

Beat the egg yolks and caster sugar until light and creamy and then fold in the almonds, lemon zest and cinnamon.

Beat the egg whites until they form firm peaks and then fold into the mixture until well incorporated.

Grease the cake tin and dust with flour, then pour the mixture in, smoothing the surface.

Bake in a moderate oven for forty-five minutes. Check with a skewer and if not cooked through, leave for another five to ten minutes.

Allow to cool, then turn out and dust liberally with the icing sugar.

Flam de Taronja
Flan de Naranja/Orange Flan

Flan must be the archetypal Spanish dessert, though the name has confused many a tourist. It is a version of crème caramel or caramel custard and this Mallorcan variation uses local orange juice instead of milk. It is usually made in ramekins to produce an individual serving, but you can use a cake tin or even a specialist *flanera*, and cut it into portions.

Makes 6 Servings

300g/10oz white granulated sugar
4 large free-range eggs
300ml/10fl oz of natural orange juice
2 tablespoons of lemon juice

Stand the ramekins in a baking tray filled with very hot water.

Place 200g/7oz of the sugar and the water in a heavy-based pan and stir over a low heat until the sugar melts and forms an amber-coloured syrup. Be careful not to let it burn. Pour an equal amount into each ramekin.

In a bowl, whisk the rest of the sugar with the eggs and then add the orange juice, mixing until well combined. Distribute evenly among the ramekins.

Tightly cover each ramekin with kitchen foil and bake in a hot oven for forty minutes - if you are using a single container, you will need about an hour.

Take the ramekins out of the water and allow to cool, then chill in the fridge overnight.

Carefully run a knife around each flan and then invert it onto a plate, allowing the caramel to run over the flan.

A Note on Food Safety

Most people understand about dates on food and ensuring that it looks and smells fresh, but there are a few other important things to remember.

Wash your hands with hot, soapy water (or ideally, bactericidal soap) before and after handling food.

To avoid cross-contamination, always thoroughly clean and sanitize the knife and preparation surface that you have used for raw food before using it for ready-to-eat food, e.g. ham, salads, cheese or bread etc. Always be aware of the possibility of the spread of harmful bacteria via utensils, washing-up equipment, cloths and towels.

When cooking or reheating food, if you have a thermometer, ensure it reaches 75°c in the centre or otherwise, be certain that it is piping hot throughout. This is particularly important when cooking chicken.

Do not leave perishable items out of the 'fridge for more than two hours.

Thaw or marinate food in the 'fridge, not at room temperature.

Always store raw meat, poultry and fish, thoroughly wrapped, at the bottom of the 'fridge to avoid dripping onto other foodstuffs.

By the same author:

Tapas
The little dishes of Spain Vol 1

Tapas
The little dishes of Spain Vol 2

The Beers of Mallorca
A comprehensive guide to the craft brewers of the island

The Diaries 2016 – 2020
An Englishman abroad in the Iberian Peninsula

Spain in the Pennines
The Tale of The Tapas Bar

In preparation:

The Wines of Mallorca

Tapas
The little dishes of Spain Vol 3

Petiscos
The little dishes of Portugal

Keep up to date at fredericksleap.com

See more about Mallorcan food and drink at atasteofmallorca.com and find recipes and information about Spanish food, restaurants and suppliers at foodsofspain.co.uk

Printed in Great Britain
by Amazon

46107207R00053